CRYPTOCURRENCY REMOTE VIEWED

BOOK TWO

KIWI JOE

ALSO IN THE REMOTE VIEWED SERIES

Cryptocurrency Remote Viewed : The Top Twelve

Cryptocurrency Remote Viewed : Book Seven

Cryptocurrency Remote Viewed : Book Six

Cryptocurrency Remote Viewed : Book Five

Cryptocurrency Remote Viewed : Book Four

Cryptocurrency Remote Viewed : Book Three

Cryptocurrency Remote Viewed : Book Two

Cryptocurrency Remote Viewed: Book One

Book One (eBook only) is *FREE* to download!

Most Secret Weapons of Nations Remote Viewed

Fukushima Radiation Solution Remote Viewed : Engineering an End to the Radioactive Leak

Forrest Fenn's Treasure Remote Viewed : The Location

Forrest Fenn's Treasure Remote Viewed : The Chest

Copyright © 2020 by Kiwi Joe.

All rights reserved.

No part of this book may be reproduced in any form or by any electronic or mechanical means, including information storage and retrieval systems, without written permission from the author, except for the use of brief quotations in a book review.

ISBN: 978-0-6485680-5-6

CONTENTS

Introduction	vii
1. Reading the Data with Ease	1
2. How we do this: Horizen	13
3. MX Token (MX)	20
4. Horizen (ZEN)	30
5. Mimblewimblecoin (MWC)	40
6. Yearn.Finance (YFI)	50
7. Steem (STEEM)	60
8. Augur (REP)	69
9. Bitcoin (BTC)	80
10. GXChain (GXC)	91
11. Conclusions	102
Notes	105
Also by Kiwi Joe	107
Also by Kiwi Joe	109
Bibliography	125

INTRODUCTION

I have to admit, the moment I realized I had just remote viewed Bitcoin, it felt like the Matrix had thrown me a curveball. Once I saw the cue after completing the session and analysis, my conclusion felt almost too black and white. After all, Bitcoin is the best-known cryptocurrency in the world.

So, did Bitcoin pan out the way maximalists expect? We will find out in Chapter Nine.

Remote viewers call the prompt a cue. In plain terms, it is the search question assigned to the target. The cue defines the nature of the query with precision, narrowing the range of data collected so that it includes only what is necessary to determine an answer.

Later in this book, I explain how we remote view

without knowing the cue in advance. It is standard practice for a remote viewer to work a target without knowing its identity. Usually, the preference is to work a session completely blind. There are occasions when a remote viewer begins with full knowledge of the target, but that generally happens only under specific conditions. In the next chapter, I explain how we work a session blind to the target.

Every crypto project I remote viewed for this series comes from the same blind target pool. It contains some 190 targets assembled from the top-ranked projects captured on October 28, 2020. The larger number of targets reduces serial dependence, where successful hits shrink the pool and increase the probability of correct guesses. A larger, more diverse target pool helps minimize this bias.

A further technical note: reliability in remote-viewing sessions depends far more on methodological rigor, target quality, and evaluation techniques than on the size of the target pool.

Remote viewing is a learned skill that harnesses human intuition, something all of us possess to some degree. For most people, it shows up in daily life simply as intuition. Many of us have experienced strange moments of synchronicity when, for no obvious reason, someone we know springs to mind. Then the phone rings, and suddenly we are speaking to the very person we had just been thinking about.

There are many variations of this. People often laugh it off and call it coincidence, as though it were merely chance. Remote viewers understand such moments differently. We see them as glimpses of an ability we are born with, one that can be strengthened through training. I discussed this ability, and how remote viewers adapt and harness it, in *Forrest Fenn's Treasure Remote Viewed: The Chest*.

In this book, I will assume you already know something about cryptocurrency and that you have read the previous volume in the series. If you have not read it yet, please grab your copy. The ebook edition of Book One is currently free to download.

In Book One, I explain the approach I take throughout this series. I discuss why I write primarily for HODLers rather than day traders. HODL is commonly taken to mean "Hold On for Dear Life," the approach favored by those who believe it is ultimately more beneficial to accumulate cryptocurrency than to trade it. In Book One, I also explain how I measure success and failure for a crypto project and describe my overall approach to remote viewing cryptocurrency.

Remote viewers refer to the information collected during a session as data, and I will use that term from this point forward. This book contains eight data chapters, one for each crypto project I remote viewed. Each chapter begins with a short overview of the project, including the price in U.S. dollars at the time of writing, a brief history of the project, and links to more technical resources.

From there, we move into the remote-viewing data. The analysis begins with two key sketches from the session. I break down the data, which includes both drawings and written impressions. I describe it, explain how I interpret it, then present a summary and draw my conclusions.

All conclusions in this book are drawn solely from my analysis of the remote-viewing data, and from nothing else. I regard that raw data as the most important part of the book. In a sense, I treat it as something akin to insider knowledge.

You may not agree with my analysis. You may find that I have given a thumbs-down to your favorite coin. You are free to conduct your own analysis using the tools I provide, together with your own specialist knowledge and informed perspective. By connecting the dots as you see them, you may discover relationships I missed. Whether you have a background in blockchain technology or simply a passion for researching crypto, your knowledge may help you recognize connections I may have overlooked. If doing your own analysis is not for you, you will still have mine to fall back on, along with my considered conclusions.

At the back of the book is a summary listing the winners and losers, that is, the long-term outlook for each crypto asset I remote viewed. I am interested in outcomes for long-term investors rather than in the valleys and peaks that occur along the way. That said, I assume a successful project will tend to show a pattern of shallower drawdowns and higher highs over time.

The aim of this series is to demonstrate how the practical application of remote viewing can provide answers to real-world questions. Remote viewing is a method of collecting data that would otherwise be difficult to obtain by other available means.

For readers who want to learn more, I include a reference list in the back matter.

If you decide you would like to learn this skill, you are going to need a teacher. While I am not available to teach remote viewing, my email address appears at the back of the book should you have questions about either the data or the analysis. I also welcome suggestions on how I might improve the series. Do not worry. I have thick skin.

One final point to keep in mind is that what you are looking at in these pages is raw remote-viewing data. For better or worse, it is presented exactly as it was captured and recorded during each

1
READING THE DATA WITH EASE

The raw data I present for each of the eight cryptocurrencies is, in my view, the most important content in this book. Raw data must be interpreted in order to make sense of it and to draw logical conclusions. In this chapter, I show you how to connect data points in ways that reveal relationships. If you prefer, you can leave the analysis to me. I provide my conclusions at the end of each data chapter.

Following protocol ensures that data is recorded as efficiently and as objectively as possible. The strictly limited time allowed for a session also reduces the opportunity for a remote viewer to become distracted. To further limit mistakes and optimize results, the viewer usually works alone and always in a room free of distractions.

Remote viewers tend to interpret data through the lens of their own perception, and that perception is shaped largely by life experience. The interests of a nuclear physicist may overlap with what catches the eye of a nuclear engineer, yet both may miss features that would stand out immediately to a fisherman or a software developer. Over time, we become specialized in one field or another, and that experience helps frame how we perceive what is in front of us.

When it comes to analyzing cryptocurrencies, my own life experience may not serve the analysis as well as firsthand knowledge of blockchain technology, coding, or information technology would. Even if that is your background, I urge you to read this chapter carefully. If you think you understand the data better than I do, then by all means trust your judgment. At the same time, consider the points I make here. My analysis, and especially my explanation of the remote-viewing data, should help you interpret what you see on the page. Even so, the raw data I captured remains the most significant contribution I have made to this book.

The Cue

One of the key elements of learning to remote view is learning how to frame the question that defines the session. That question is called the **Cue**. By design, a cue focuses on the specific information needed and filters out anything that would confuse the session. Like a precise request in a vast library, a cue is carefully constructed so that it returns a useful answer.

A new cue is tested first to confirm that its results are reliable. No matter how skilled a remote viewer may be, if the right question is not asked, the answer will be useless.

Because the cue is specific, all **Site Template** data, often referred to as the **ST**, is considered relevant to the inquiry. The ST is one of two key sketches included in each chapter, and I explain both below. Learning how to cue properly is a skill that takes time and practice to master. Cues can be proprietary, and the most prized ones are sometimes handed down from teacher to trusted student.

Being Blind to the Target

A remote viewer is usually, though not always, blind to the target while working a session. A session begins with a unique sequence of randomly generated numbers, or a mix of numbers and letters, linked to the hidden cue. This sequence is called a **Target Reference Number**, more often referred to simply as the **TRN**.

A TRN is divided into two parts by a slash mark. It functions as a key that allows the remote viewer to access data. Because the remote viewer typically does not know the cue until the session is complete, the viewer is effectively blindfolded while collecting and recording data. This helps support reliable results.

That is how a session works when the remote viewer is completely blind to the target. At the start, all the viewer sees is the number sequence. In the data chapters, the TRN appears in the upper-left corner of the ST sketch page and on the S6 page that follows.

The Matrix

Remote viewers consider the data to come from what they call the **Matrix**. This has nothing to do with the movies of the same name. The Matrix can be imagined as a vast, decentralized library surrounding us. It contains all information that has ever existed, and all that will exist. This conception is similar to the proverbial ether. It is not presented here, however, as mysticism or magic.

Remote viewers consider the Matrix explainable in terms of the material world. Put another way, remote viewing targets reality, whether that reality involves a life form, an inanimate object, a concept, or even the thoughts of others. Traditional science, as taught in universities, has historically struggled with the reality of remote viewing.

When we tap into the Matrix for data, we do so by way of what remote viewers call the **Signal Line.** Since science has not yet conclusively demonstrated the existence of the Signal Line, it remains theoretical, just like the Matrix. As well-known remote viewer Lyn Buchanan dryly describes it, remote viewers use these terms to "look semi-intelligent," but what they are really saying is, "I don't know where the information comes from."[1] If you want to explore these foundational concepts in greater depth, consult the titles in the reference list at the back of this book.

The Analytical Sketches

As mentioned above, a remote viewer begins a session with the TRN. From there, the viewer follows a well-practiced series of steps within a limited time frame until completing a base session and establishing the ST. The second sketch is the S6 page. For the purposes of this series, it is the final sketch completed.

Analyzing the remote-viewing data means describing and explaining the information assembled in the sketches. You may be disappointed by their minimalist appearance and by the overall lack of detail. One reason is the time constraint imposed by remote-viewing protocol, which allows only simple line drawings.

The ST page takes the longest time to complete in the base session, and there is only so much detail that can be included within a short time frame. This also means that everything you see in the sketches is relevant to the analysis.

Because the sketches leading up to the ST are drawn quickly, simple archetypes are favored over detailed features. Even so, interactions between aspects and elements are included whenever they appear in the data. The archetypes used in this book include the following:

- Right angles indicate man-made structures.
- Arrows indicate a vector. For our purposes, a vector means a directional force. My apologies to the physics folks who will be disappointed that mine do not include magnitude. Vectors indicate the direction of movement, such as water or air currents. In this book, they often show the direction of light or electrical energy from a source. Usually, the nature of the aspects, and the

way they relate to one another in the ST, makes it clear what the arrows represent.
- Diagonal crosshatched lines indicate a solid mass. These should not be confused with perspective indicators, which are larger crosshatched lines that fan out from a distant horizon.[2]

Site Template

The Site Template, or ST, is a full page sketch that is the culmination of the base remote-viewing session. This page contains the most complex sketch in the session. It brings together the objects the data describes, referred to from here on as Aspects. In this series, I limit each session to just three aspects. The ST, then, lays out the aspects of the particular cryptocurrency targeted by the remote-viewing session.

The page contains all aspects explored during that session. The targeted item in the ST, called Aspect X, is colored for easy identification.[3] The other two aspects are titled Aspect A and Aspect B. The text data in the ST, and in the breakdown of each aspect that follows, is capitalized.

Even if the ST appears abstract, you are looking at

three key aspects of the targeted cryptocurrency. It is important to understand that the Matrix does not care whether the information it reveals is officially available to the public. It may even be the case that those behind a project would prefer the public not recognize what the ST shows. The Matrix reveals whatever data is relevant to the cue. It is up to the remote viewer to capture that data and record it transparently. It may even reveal something critical to a project that the developers themselves are unaware of.

Remote viewers quickly learn that, when it comes to data, it is what it is. Remote viewing deals with truth, no matter how unpalatable that truth may turn out to be. Treat whatever you see in the ST as important.

S6

Once the ST is complete, a remote viewer can probe for additional information in a follow-up stage, and that is where the second full page sketch comes in. The S6 contains higher-level attributes, the nature of which depends on the inquiry. The focus may be a particular aspect in the ST, or it may be the entire ST. The session may look to the past to determine the cause of an event, or it may probe for a future outcome.

For the purposes of this series, the S6 is the final sketch completed, and it contains the data that determines the ultimate success or failure of the cryptocurrency in question.

In this series, the S6 probes the ST to predict the ultimate outcome for the cryptocurrency targeted in the ST. Specifically, I focus on whether the project ultimately succeeds or fails. The data in an S6 is higher-level information. It may be the answer you want, and it may not, but it is always what it is.

Here, I aim to predict the fate of the targeted crypto projects. In other words, I want to ascertain what we construe as a future event. From the perspective of the Matrix, it has already occurred. That is about as woo-woo as I want to get here, and it may be the hardest idea in the chapter for some readers to digest. The rest of the chapter is more straightforward by comparison.

Sensories

Sensories are pieces of text data associated with a particular aspect in the ST. In general, sensories include things, concepts, and symbols. They may be a single word, but they are often phrases. I present them in two groups. In one group, words and phrases are capitalized. In the other, they are not.

When sensories are capitalized in a sketch, they are also capitalized in the analysis that follows. This text data should be considered as significant as the drawn aspects.

You will also see text in the analysis that does not appear in capitals and is not written in the sketches. This data describes what the remote viewer experiences. Although the remote viewer is not physically at the target site, the sensations are experienced and recorded during the session as though they were firsthand. These are secondary sensories compared with the capitalized terms and phrases, but they are no less valuable.

In this series, I group secondary sensories into categories such as color and other qualities of light, movement, sound, dimensions, positioning, and weight. Not all of these appear in every session.

Quotation marks enclosing words or phrases indicate text that is overheard or seen, for example, a company name seen on the side panel of a truck.

Words or phrases preceded by letter combinations are remote-viewing acronyms. The acronyms used in this series include the following.

In remote viewing, **AI** is an acronym for an

emotion felt by the remote viewer. Here, AI does not mean artificial intelligence. It describes how the viewer is affected by an aspect while capturing the data. An aspect may look relatively innocuous on the page, and the written data may present it as harmless, even though the viewer's experience of it was distinctly unpleasant. The emotional impact can reveal something about an aspect's function or role. That is why the emotion is recorded on the ST as an AI.

The remote viewer considers the AI when analyzing the data. An AI is not always present among the sensories associated with an aspect, but it is common to see it recorded in the ST. There is a second type of emotion recorded in the ST, and it should not be confused with AI.

An **EI** indicates the emotion felt by at least one life form associated with the site. An EI entered in the ST when a life form is not drawn indicates that a life form is present in association with the ST, even if it is not visible in the sketch.

In summary, an AI records the emotion felt by the remote viewer when encountering an aspect during the session. An EI records the emotion felt by a life form associated with the ST and, by default, also indicates that a life form has been detected at the site. Take care not to confuse AI with EI.

AOL and AOL/S

You will not see an AOL in the data, but it needs to be mentioned here. An AOL is a recurring idea recorded during the session that comes from imagination. The remote viewer follows a procedure to label it and clear it so that it does not corrupt the data. Students are taught early in their training how to recognize AOLs and reject them. AOLs are a product of the analytic mind attempting to interpret the data as a remembered thing.

I mention AOLs for two reasons. First, to reassure readers that remote viewers are fully aware of the threat posed by imagination. If the analytic mind intrudes without being addressed during a session, it can render raw data nonsensical or distract from the real data coming from the Matrix.

Second, I want to introduce an important sensory known as an **AOL/S.** This is an AOL that occurs repeatedly, no matter how the remote viewer attempts to clear it by following protocol. Once an idea is identified as an AOL/S, the viewer treats it as a clear indication that a strong connection has been established with the Signal Line. The sensory is recorded during the session, prefixed with AOL/S, and included in the ST as significant data.

2

HOW WE DO THIS: HORIZEN

I will assume you have read Book One and are already familiar with the key concepts and terminology. In this chapter, I show you how to analyze remote-viewing data. The process is methodical and works best when approached step by step. I highlight the specific features to look for during analysis. Watch for patterns in the data, because they are always revealing.

Chapter Four, *Horizen*, demonstrates what remote-viewing data can reveal about a target. When analyzing a session from scratch, the first step is identification. Identify everything you can. Next, explain how those elements fit together and how they relate to one another. Finally, draw conclusions. That final step matters most. If you reach the end without conclusions, it usually means the earlier steps were incomplete.

Keep in mind that the cue initiating each session was designed to answer a specific question: will the targeted crypto ultimately fail or succeed?

Treat the sketches as raw data. The ST page comes first, followed by the S6 page. Once the ST is complete, we can probe for more specific information using a variety of approaches. For the purposes of this series, the approach I use is the S6. The ST anchors the S6.

The S6 is designed to answer the larger question: does the crypto ultimately fail or succeed? You might reasonably ask why, if the goal is to determine whether the cryptocurrency is a winner or a loser, and the S6 delivers that answer, I bother analyzing the ST at all.

The answer is that the ST is an important part of the story. It pulls back the cover on the cryptocurrency project itself. Some readers will have deeper knowledge of blockchain technology than I do. For those readers, the ST may reveal additional meaning and context that I miss.

In the brief analysis beneath the sketches, I describe what I see and how it all fits together. That includes relationships within an aspect, as well as relationships between aspects. Overall, the analysis moves from the general to the specific. The ST is assembled at the higher level of aspects. For the purposes of this series, I limit the investigation to three: Aspect X, Aspect A, and Aspect B.

Each aspect may contain more than one feature. Features are associated with text data entered on the sketch page. That text data is capitalized on the sketch page and carried into the analysis below it.

The analysis also includes sensories such as size, movement, color, and other descriptive impressions in the form of a word or phrase. Sensories are not capitalized and, depending on whether they are primary or secondary, do not all appear on the sketch page.

Aspect X is always the target, and in both the ebook and print editions I have colorized it for easy identification. If the data does not specify a color for the aspect, I color it to match the crypto's logo. Coloring Aspect X is not part of remote-viewing protocol.

Aspects A and B follow, and the same method applies. The capitalized words and phrases visible in the sketch are carried into the analysis below. Sensories are then added to describe each feature more fully and to fill out the picture.

The Analysis Steps

These are the steps I use in analysis:

1 Identify the data.[1]

2 Describe the data.

3 Explain the data.

4 Draw conclusions from the data.

A remote viewer arrives at a target with no knowledge of what it is, and usually with no sense of where they are in relation to it. In most cases, the viewer begins the session completely blind to the target. At first, the viewer learns about it only as the data comes in. The viewpoint can be anything, including a perspective inside or outside an object, whether minuscule or vast.

A viewer might find themselves inside a human body, observing a problem at the cellular level. They might be floating in hot, swirling gas clouds, looking down at the surface of Venus from a thousand feet above. They might be standing inside a foreign missile-launch facility. They might be in a dry wilderness, searching for a vein of silver beneath their feet.

The Matrix does not provide signposts. Protocol helps the viewer navigate the target. The viewer's first task is to determine what the target is and what to make of the surroundings. Time can also be uncertain. Is the target in the present? Is it a past event? Is it something in the future?

In these sessions, time is not the issue. All you need

to know here is that the S6 shows the crypto's future state.

An Issue of Displacement

Another issue to be aware of is displacement within the ST. This can occur while the remote viewer is assembling the ST during a session. Note that I am not referring here to the separate issue also called displacement that often confronts viewers using Associated Remote Viewing. I will not go into that methodology here.[2]

Establishing how features within a ST relate to one another can be tricky. See the section titled "Comparing the ST with Horizen's Official Website Animation" in Chapter Four. There you will see an image, shown in color in the ebook or in grayscale in print, of a center plate that closely resembles what appears in the website animation, though it is also slightly, yet still distinctly, displaced.

In the Horizen session, I may have targeted the website animation itself, or I may have targeted the concept the animation represents. If it is the former, then my sketch and the professional artist's animation are simply two different representations of the same targeted concept. When I compare my ST sketch to the animation, I see strong similarities in aspects and features, even if their positioning differs. In that case, displacement is the simplest explanation.

Aspects in a target are recorded as accurately as possible. The ST can then be probed for more data in order to determine details with greater precision.

What I Look for to Determine Success or Failure

When determining whether the data points to future success for a project, I look for clear signs of utility. I do not look for symbols of increasing value, such as stacks of money or bars of gold. If that kind of imagery does appear in the S6, I accept that the crypto may return a profit to those invested in it. Even so, what I look for most is activity in the S6, and that usually appears as movement. I want to see action, especially the busting-out and growth kind. In other words, I look for energy.

I also look for signs that the lights are on. I expect brightness, whether as a glow, a shine, or some kind of glare. As we saw in Books One and Two, light may even take the form of a flash or an explosion. I look for a buzz, meaning excitement or outright happiness. I look for vibrancy, general busyness, enterprise, production, and movement to and fro. I also look for signs of life, such as people present in the S6 or people clearly associated with it.

For failure, I look for the opposite. I do not want to see a notable absence of light and action. Failure tends to show darkness rather than light, and stillness rather than action. There may be signs of demise, such as indications of a crash or plunge with no apparent comeback. In short, there may be a notable absence of life in both the ST and the S6. There may also be emotional residue, such as sadness, anger, disbelief, or related reactions that follow the sinking or implosion of a crypto project. These are indicators of failure that generally appear in the S6 if that is the fate of the targeted project.

If a targeted crypto is going to fail in the future, that will usually be clear in the data. Otherwise, failure may be implied by the absence of indicators of success. It also follows that a project that does not fail may still succeed to varying degrees. When I find ambiguity in the S6, I add words of caution in my conclusion.

The data chapters that follow are ordered by the date and time I completed the remote-viewing sessions. If you have a background in blockchain technology, or in IT more broadly, begin by re-identifying my raw data before attempting to interpret it.

3

MX TOKEN (MX)

About MX Token

Price in USD: $0.158534

Market Cap: $24,037,467

Circulating Supply: 151,623,448 (23.98% of the total supply).

[Date and Source: 04:45 UTC Tuesday, 24 November 2020; https://coinmarketcap.com/]

White Paper (from here on referred to as 'WP'): https://www.mxc.org/documents/MXC_data_economy_whitepaper.pdf

Official Website: https://www.mxc.com/

Background of MX Token

MX is the native token of the MEXC exchange, a digital-asset trading platform launched in 2018. MEXC describes its platform as a multi-cluster, high-performance exchange and says its trading engine can process up to 1.4 million transactions per second. The platform supports trading in many cryptocurrencies and offers multilingual customer support. MEXC also announced that it won the title "Best Crypto Exchange in Asia" at Crypto Expo Dubai 2021.

MX is built on Ethereum as an ERC-20 token. According to CoinMarketCap, MX holders may receive benefits such as voting rights, participation in community activities and promotions, trading-fee use cases, and access to MX DeFi mining. Public information on the token is available through exchange materials and market-data sites, and independent reviews of MEXC can also be found online.[1]

Let's move on to the remote-viewing data for this target.

ST - MX Token

The ST for this session is as follows.

MX TOKEN (MX) 23

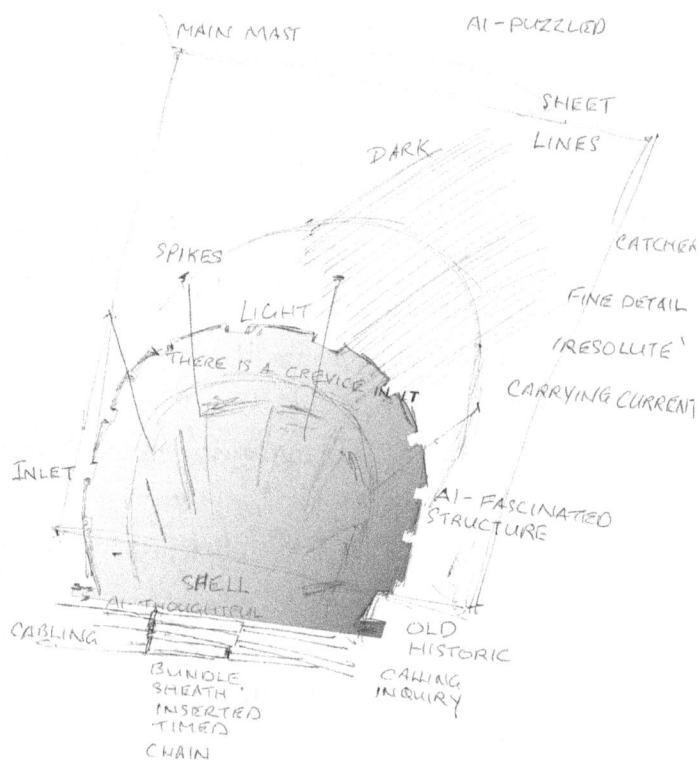

Overview of the ST Sketch

The ST consists of three main aspects. All STs in this book explore only three aspects, in order to stay within the scope of the project. Remember, the aim of every coin chapter is to reach a conclusion about the future success or failure of each cryptocurrency.

For the purpose of this book, the ST is the foundation that leads us to the S6. In line with the cue I constructed, the S6 provides the data needed to determine the project's ultimate success or failure. However, because the ST captures a largely conceptual target, it often presents a complex mix of aspects and elements. For that reason, the ST can also offer insights into the cryptocurrency project itself.

• Aspect X resembles a scallop shell and is colored black in the eBook edition (gray in print).

• Aspect A looks like a bundle of rods that lies at the base of Aspect X.

• Aspect B is a large angular object with diagonal lines running down one corner. It appears to sit behind Aspect X.

Aspect X

A big, thick, curved, open STRUCTURE with SPIKES, colored black, is associated with INLET, OLD, HISTORIC, and SHELL. There is also the idea: THERE IS A CREVICE IN IT.

I feel FASCINATED.

Aspect A

A heavy, angular BUNDLE in the form of a shiny SHEATH that is thin and long, with small features, is associated with INSERTED, CABLING, CHAIN, TIMED, and INQUIRY.

I feel THOUGHTFUL.

Aspect B

A black, wide, curved SHEET that is flat across, DARK toward the top and LIGHT toward the bottom, with thin, straight LINES, is associated with CATCHER and "RESOLUTE." There are also the ideas of MAIN MAST, FINE DETAIL, and CARRYING CURRENT.

I feel PUZZLED.

Comments on the ST

I invite you to do your own analysis of the data, especially if you have experience in IT, the blockchain industry, or specific knowledge of MX Token. With deeper knowledge of the target, you may recognize elements I did not. It is also possible that I misdescribed certain features as I translated sketch data into words. If you can bring domain knowledge to the raw data, you may glean insights I miss.

S6 - The Ultimate Future of MX Token

The final page of data from the remote viewing session follows.

63457/70779   SG

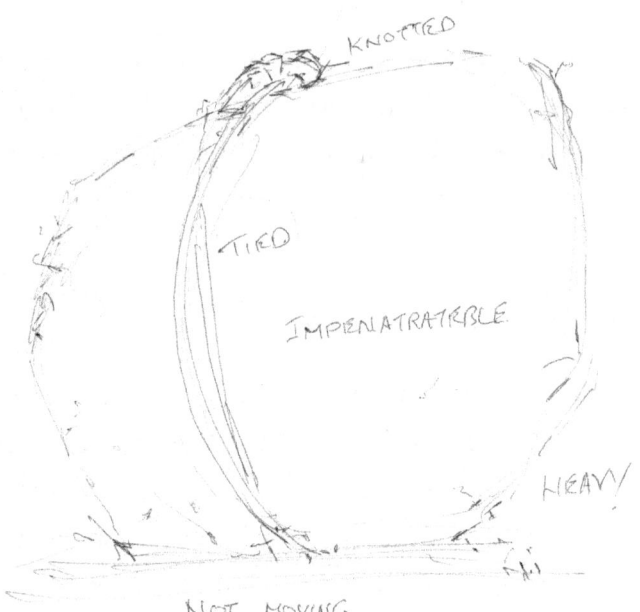

KNOTTED
TIED
IMPENATRATRBLE
HEAVY
NOT MOVING
LIKE A ROCK!

KIWI
SESSION END @ 07:47 AEST
17 NOVEMBER 2020

The text data from the S6:

It is LIKE A ROCK.

It is IMPENETRABLE (spelling corrected from the session) and HEAVY.

It is TIED and KNOTTED.

It is NOT MOVING.

The object sits on a base or platform, giving it the appearance of a sculpture or statue. In short, the S6 object resembles a monolith. It appears fixed and lifeless.

Comments and Conclusions on the S6

The lack of movement is not a good sign. In fact, the data presents iconic imagery that amounts to the equivalent of a stop sign at the end of the road.

The image of a rock tied with what appears to be a knotted rope reminds me of the iconic *tome-ishi* in Japan. The direct translation is "stop stone." It is a rock tied with a knotted rope or cord and placed in a path to symbolize "no entry." The function is to keep people on the correct path. It is also called *sekimori ishi*, the meaning of which is "boundary guard-stone." Both Japanese names translate more simply as "Stop."

Continuing with Japanese symbolism, thick ropes made from rice straw are often found in and around

Shinto shrines. They mark boundaries between what is regarded as sacred and what is considered profane. These ropes are sometimes tied around trees, and often around large stones or other stone objects.

Setting Japanese imagery aside, the object in the S6 also suggests an ancient anchor, so again we see the functions of holding something in place. The sensories "Heavy" and "Not moving" support that comparison.

My Conclusion for MX Token

The sensory "Impenetrable" may be the key to unlocking the puzzle. In the context of the tied rock, the meaning can be read as closed and isolated. It can also simultaneously mean incorruptible and secure. This interpretation points to a desirable strength.

However, I am worried by the absence of positive indicators such as action, light, and people. I am left with the impression that MX Token is a project that will not be judged successful in the future.

Based on the S6 data alone, this project is not a keeper.

4
HORIZEN (ZEN)

About Horizen

Price in USD: $12.80

Market Cap: $133,622,085

Circulating Supply: 10,441,575 (49.72% of the total supply).

[Date and Source: 04:45 UTC Tuesday, 24 November 2020; https://coinmarketcap.com/]

WP: https://www.horizen.io/research/

Official Website: https://www.horizen.io/

Background of Horizen

Horizen launched in 2017 with a strong community-focused mission aimed at empowering individuals around the world. The project was originally known as ZenCash, and its native token is ZEN. Official Horizen materials currently identify Sphere primarily as the project's wallet application, while also highlighting Zendoo as Horizen's customizable sidechain protocol.

Zendoo extends the network's capabilities by supporting customizable blockchains and cross-chain functionality. Horizen Academy also provides free educational resources for readers interested in blockchain technology and Web3.

Let's move on to the remote viewing data for this target.

ST — Horizen

The Site Template (ST) for this session follows.

94682/98024 S1

- AI-STARTLED
- CHUTE
- PIPE
- CALLING
- DIRECTED
- FLARING OUT
- AI-FASCINATED
- BUTTONS
- INNER CORE
- RIM
- DISH
- OPEN
- CAPTURING
- RENDERING
- DELIVERING
- INNOCUOUS
- AI-CLAUSTROPHOBIC
- AOL/S – SPHERE
- AMPLIFYING
- TRAPPING IT
- RESONATING
- STORING
- FLASK
- CONTAINER

MEASURING TIME

Overview of the ST Sketch

Aspect X

Aspect X is colored purple with an orange core in the eBook edition (gray in print). This is the target aspect. It resembles the spreading cap of a mushroom.

The target aspect is an open, shallow, coppery, purple-colored DISH with a wide, curved RIM. It is associated with INNOCUOUS, CAPTURING, RENDERING, and DELIVERING. There is also the idea of INNER CORE.

I feel FASCINATED.

Aspect A

Aspect A is a long, thin, horizontal structure positioned directly above Aspect X, with force indicated by an arrow moving from west to east.

Aspect A is a white CHUTE, a hollow, narrow PIPE. Something moves quickly along it. The aspect is associated with DIRECTED, CALLING, STIPPLED, and BUTTONS. There is the idea of FLARING OUT.

I feel STARTLED.

· · ·

Aspect B

Aspect B forms the stalk-like structure beneath the cap, including a spread at the base and an open, horseshoe-shaped form at the center.

I cannot shake the recurring idea of SPHERE.

There is a deep, tall, OPEN cylindrical CONTAINER, a FLASK. It is associated with RESONATING, AMPLIFYING, and STORING. There are also the ideas of TRAPPING IT and MEASURING TIME.

I feel CLAUSTROPHOBIC.

Comparing the ST with Horizen's Official Website Animation

The compiled images from Horizen's official animation show the project in action. When comparing the animation with the ST, several similarities stand out, along with a few intriguing differences.

This graphic consists of frames compiled from the original animation on Horizen's website to better show the step-like levels at the base of the chain. See the endnote for a link to the original animation on the Horizen website.

In the ST, the inner circular plate appears above the larger open circular element shaped like a horseshoe. In the official animation, that plate is positioned inside the horseshoe structure, not above it. Similarly, the ST presents step-like lines arranged on a circular feature, whereas the animation places them on angular architecture. Even so, the number and orientation of the steps, particularly on the southwest corner, align closely with the animation.

The chute-like structure with its directed "calling," represented by Aspect A, does not appear in the official graphic at all. That absence makes it even more interesting. If I were to conduct follow-up remote viewing, I would begin with this element. What is it? What does it do? And why does it matter to Horizen?

S6 — The Ultimate Future of Horizen

The S6 data presents a dynamic, intense set of impressions:

HORIZEN (ZEN) 37

99682/98024. S6.
HAVE COURAGE!
MOMENTUM UP TOP.
BUILT UP

FIERY.
BRIGHT COLORS.
REDS
ORANGES
BLUES

BIG
EXPANDING

WISEMEN SAY!
"RECKLESS" THEY SAY
SOME DANGER BELOW
"MADNESS!"

KIWI.
SESSION END @ 19:15 AEST
17 NOV. 2020

The text data from the S6:

HAVE COURAGE!

There is MOMENTUM UP TOP.

There is BUILD-UP.

There is an anti-clockwise spiraling movement on the horizontal axis.

It is FIERY.

There are several BRIGHT COLORS, including notable REDS, ORANGES, and BLUES.

It is BIG and EXPANDING.

Voices of WISE MEN SAY:

"RECKLESS."

"SOME DANGER BELOW."

"MADNESS!"

A large structure exhibits upward momentum, supported by build-up and block-like formations reminiscent of urban density. The spiral at the center echoes the form and coloration of Aspect X from the ST. The fiery palette and expansive movement point toward rapid growth and increased adoption.

The warnings, "Reckless," "Danger below," and "Madness," suggest a mix of excitement and apprehension surrounding the project's trajectory.

Comments and Conclusions on the S6

The S6 data portrays a cryptocurrency gaining energy, urgency, and widespread interest. The imagery of fiery expansion, combined with the call to "Have courage," signals strong forward momentum. The structure is described as having build-up, suggesting robust foundations, while the sense of movement "up top" reinforces the idea of large-scale growth.

There are cautions as well, including warnings of danger and accusations of recklessness. These suggest risk, volatility, or surprising developments that may accompany growth.

Even so, the overall impression points to a project with momentum, impact, and potential for significant value appreciation.

Based on the combined ST and S6 data, I conclude that Horizen is a keeper.

MIMBLEWIMBLECOIN (MWC)

About Mimblewimblecoin

Price in USD: $5.70

Market Cap: $60,815,585

Circulating Supply: 10,669,622 (53.35% of the total supply).

[Date and Source: 04:45 UTC Tuesday, 24 November 2020; https://coinmarketcap.com/]

WP: https://www.mwc.mw/whitepaper

Official Website: https://www.mwc.mw/

Background of Mimblewimblecoin

Mimblewimble emerged in 2016 in a white paper published under the pseudonym Tom Elvis Jedusor, a reference to a magical spell in the *Harry Potter* series. Although both Mimblewimble and Bitcoin began under pseudonyms, the similarity largely ends there.

The protocol is generally described as more privacy-focused and more scalable than Bitcoin's design. Mimblewimble transactions do not record addresses on-chain; instead, they use cryptographic commitments and blinding factors so that transaction details are obscured while still verifiable. Projects built on the protocol include Grin and Beam, both of which launched mainnet in January 2019.

MimbleWimbleCoin (MWC) is a separate cryptocurrency built on the Mimblewimble protocol. According to the project's website, MWC has a supply cap of 20,000,000 coins and is designed as a pure Proof-of-Work coin emphasizing scalability, privacy, and fungibility. The project also presents MWC as a complement to Bitcoin rather than a replacement for it.

Let's move on to the remote viewing data for this target.

ST - Mimblewimblecoin

The Site Template for this session follows.

MIMBLEWIMBLECOIN (MWC)   43

81172/87326   ST.

AI - EXCITED   FUTURISTIC DESIGN
BEIGE   FOCUS POINT   LIGHT YEARS
APPARATUS
CONTROL   BLACK.
HIGHLY ADJUSTABLE   FLAT PLATES
SANDWICH   STAGING PLATFORM   PROVIDING JUMPING OVER POINTS
        LOOKS LESS THAN WHAT IT IS

BRIGHT LIGHT.
AI - AMAZED   LIFEFORM
OBJECT
ARTIFICIAL
STRUCTURE
    UPLOADED
HARDY
ENDURING
STANDING READY
SIGNIFICANT STRESS LEVELS
    READINESS

        AI - SURPRISED
        TUBE
GRATING NOISE   COIL
        WIRE
        TANGENTAL
TAKING HOLD OF IT
        WINDING DOWN TO END POINT
SMOOTHLY WORKING BACK AND FORWARD

Overview of the ST Sketch

• Aspect X is a person inside a straight-line, capsule-like space, with a pronounced bulging, curved ceiling element on one side. Aspect X is colored purple in the eBook edition (gray in print).

• Aspect A is a large tube stretching from the lower portion of the ST toward the northeast corner, with a coil running through its length.

• Aspect B is positioned directly above Aspect X and in front of Aspect A. It is angular, with a roof-like form that slopes toward the center and two separate plates on the bottom.

Aspect X

The OBJECT is a LIFE FORM inside an ARTIFICIAL STRUCTURE that is high, angular, and curved. It is associated with HARDY, ENDURING, UPLOADED, and READINESS. Additional ideas include STANDING READY, SIGNIFICANT STRESS LEVELS, and BRIGHT LIGHT.

I feel AMAZED.

. . .

Aspect A

A long, vertical, shiny, hollow BLACK TUBE containing a COIL of WIRE is associated with TANGENTIAL (spelling corrected from the session). Additional ideas include SMOOTHLY WORKING BACK AND FORTH, GRATING NOISE, TAKING HOLD OF IT, and WINDING DOWN TO AN ENDPOINT.

I feel SURPRISED.

Aspect B

Long, thin, angular FLAT PLATES in a reddish beige color are associated with SANDWICH, APPARATUS, CONTROL, and FOCUS POINT. Additional ideas include IN TWO PIECES, PROVIDING JUMP-OVER POINTS, HIGHLY ADJUSTABLE, FUTURISTIC DESIGN, LIGHT YEARS, LOOKS LESS THAN WHAT IT IS, and STAGING PLATFORM.

I feel EXCITED.

Comments on the ST

I note that my feelings when experiencing all the data are similar. I feel "amazed","surprised", and "excited". The person in the capsule appears to be operating controls that raise anxiety levels, suggesting a task that requires a high degree of concentration.

The other two aspects also suggest complex technology involving electricity. That impression is supported by the coil of wire in Aspect A, and by the flat plates and "jump-over points" in Aspect B.

S6 - The Ultimate Future of Mimblewimblecoin

The final page of data from the remote viewing session follows.

81172/87328   S6

BLOCKS OF TRANSPARENCY.

PLATES ARE LINED UP.

FLORESCENT COLORS

PEOPLE TOGETHER

GOING THROUGH AN ARCH

JOURNEY   CHANNELING!

KIWI
SESSIONS END @ 19:40 AEST
18 NOVEMBER 2020

The text data from the S6:

There are vertical BLOCKS OF TRANSPARENCY.
    The PLATES ARE LINED UP.
    There are FLUORESCENT COLORS.
    There are two PEOPLE TOGETHER.
    They are GOING THROUGH AN ARCH.
    It is a JOURNEY.
    There is CHANNELING!

Comments and Conclusions on the S6

This is rather odd stuff. There is a particular form of travel, or guided movement. The scene feels futuristic, which matches "Futuristic design," the phrase in the site template, associated with Aspect B.

There is a significant overlap with the ST, both in terms of the tunnel through the hoops, and the people moving in the same direction. They are inside a structure that moves them. The mention of 'plates' appears again in the phrase "plates are lined up".

"Channeling!" stands out in the text data because of the exclamation mark. One common use of the word refers to communication with spirit entities. Another meaning appears in physics, where channeling describes how charged particles can travel more easily along certain paths within a structured medium. The word can also simply mean directing something toward a specific end.

Taken together, "blocks of transparency," "fluorescent colors," and the rapid movement of two people through an arch in what seems like a guided device suggest practical utility. I do not see indicators of a crash, implosion, or other signs of demise for the project.

My Conclusion for Mimblewimblecoin

Even if MW's future is not a spectacular success, it looks to be steady. There is a journey involved, but we know that often enough, steady wins the race.

I conclude that MimbleWimbleCoin is a keeper.

6

YEARN.FINANCE (YFI)

About Yearn.Finance

Price in USD: $25,499.49

Market Cap: $764,162,207

Circulating Supply: 29,968 (99.89% of the total supply).

[Date and Source: 04:45 UTC Tuesday, 24 November 2020; https://coinmarketcap.com/]

WP: https://yfdot.finance/whitepaper.pdf

Official Website: https://yearn.finance/

Background of Yearn.Finance

Yearn.finance is a DeFi yield aggregator built on Ethereum. Its core product is the vault system, which automates yield-earning strategies for deposited assets. In earlier versions of the protocol, Yearn could move funds among lending markets such as Aave, dYdX, and Compound to seek better returns, reducing the need for users to juggle multiple protocols themselves.

That automation addressed one of DeFi's main friction points for lenders and yield seekers: the need to monitor several protocols and shift funds manually. Yearn's design aimed to simplify that process by routing assets through automated strategies rather than requiring constant user intervention.

YFI is Yearn.finance's governance token. Official Yearn documentation states that the original distribution involved 30,000 YFI awarded to liquidity providers in 2020. YFI rose sharply after its July 2020 launch, and its limited initial supply became a major part of the token's early market narrative.

Let's move on to the remote viewing data for this target.

ST - Yearn.Finance

The Site Template for this session follows.

YEARN.FINANCE (YFI)

42023/05188 ST

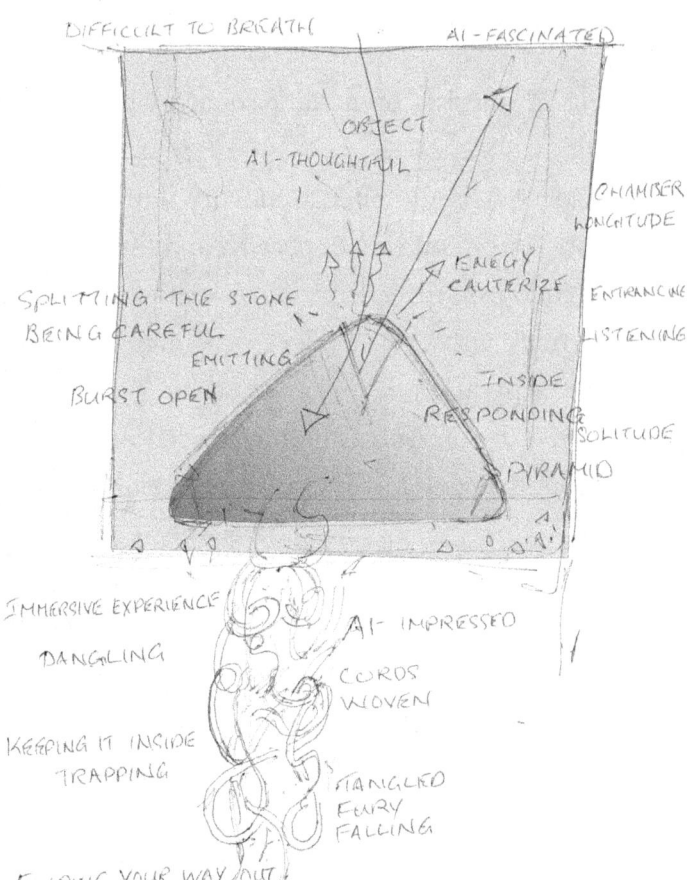

Overview of the ST Sketch

• Aspect X consists of a dark square with a triangle inside it.

• Aspect A is the energy moving into the triangle from above, from outside Aspect X, and then out again. The direction of the energy flow is shown by the two large arrows and the smaller wavy arrows from the apex of the pyramid.

• Aspect B consists of a long, tangled mass hanging down from the center of the ST to the bottom of it and beyond.

Aspect X

Inside a CHAMBER, a dense, pointed, yet curved PYRAMID is enclosed, along with scattered angular fragments on the surface. Associated with the target are these sensories: LONGITUDE, SYMBOLISM, ENTRANCING, LISTENING, and SOLITUDE. Additional ideas include DIFFICULT TO BREATHE (spelling corrected from the session) and BEING CAREFUL.

It makes me feel FASCINATED.

. . .

Aspect A

ENERGY moves down from above and into an OBJECT, and then comes out again. Associated are CAUTERIZE, EMITTING, and RESPONDING. Additional ideas include SPLITTING THE STONE, FROM ABOVE TO BELOW, and BURST OPEN.

It makes me feel THOUGHTFUL.

Aspect B

CORDS colored white, green, and red are associated with TANGLED, DANGLING, TRAPPING, and WOVEN, moving over and under, across, and in and out. They are also associated with FURY and FALLING. They are long, looped, and thin. Additional ideas include KEEPING IT INSIDE, IMMERSIVE EXPERIENCE, and FINDING YOUR WAY OUT.

I am IMPRESSED.

Comments on the ST

There is direct interaction between Aspect X and Aspect A. There is an energy exchange, with a strong flow that sweeps into Aspect X from outside the square chamber and out across the apex of the "Pyramid."

A particularly strong flow shoots from the top

toward the northeast. The exchange appears to occur near the same point where the strong current enters the top of the pyramid from outside the "Chamber."

I am not certain there is direct contact between Aspect B and the other two aspects. The way I read it, the "Cords" may represent a product of the interaction between Aspects X and A.

S6 - The Ultimate Future of Yearn.Finance

The final page of data from the remote viewing session follows.

42023/05188   S6.

NOISE
ACTION
CELEBRATION

GLASSY
GLOWING

CONTAINED

SEISMIC

"STRIFER"

SPINNING OFF FROM IT.

"SHIPS AWAY"

KIWI.
SK3FLORA END @ 05.50 AFTT
19 NOV. 2020

The text data from the S6:

There is NOISE, ACTION, and CELEBRATION.

There is a GLASSY, GLOWING semi-circle or dome that sits on the horizon.

The dome is CONTAINED on the horizontal axis.

There is SEISMIC.

I hear the word "STRIFER."

Something is SPINNING OFF FROM IT.

I hear "SHIPS AWAY," and connected with those words is a looping arrow showing rapid, tumbling movement.

On the right side of the S6, there are three circles connected by a half-circle.

There are four related features: a dome, a glow, a horizon, and three connected circles. The group is moving in a clockwise rotation.

Comments and Conclusions on the S6

The S6 suggests an ultimate future with a lot of activity and a sense of celebration, both of which are positive indicators.

"Seismic" suggests events that shake established foundations. That could be positive or negative, but I do not see anything here that reads as ominous. The overall impression is energetic and active.

However, the word "Strifer" introduces a note of uncertainty. If any reader knows what the word means in a relevant context, I would appreciate an email.

Something appears to spin off from the main flow. The phrase "Ships away" suggests a departure, as if a new journey begins. I also note that a half-circle sits at the heart of the S6 rather than a full circle. The glowing dome does resemble a rising or setting sun, but it reads more like a contained dome than a vast body such as the sun itself.

My Conclusion for Yearn.Finance

Yearn.Finance has a promising future, and the data suggests more upside ahead. At the same time, I would prepare for the possibility of a breakaway event further along, such as a spin-off or a related project that separates from the main flow.

For that reason, it would be prudent to stay alert for sudden changes, including developments that might signal a shift in fortune.

I conclude that Yearn.Finance is a keeper, at least for now.

7
STEEM (STEEM)

About Steem

Price in USD: $0.181974

Market Cap: $71,101,694

Circulating Supply: 390,723,541 (95.84% of the total supply).

[Date and Source: 04:45 UTC Tuesday, 24 November 2020; https://coinmarketcap.com/]

WP: https://steem.com/SteemWhitePaper.pdf

Official Website: https://steem.com/

Background of Steem

Steem is a blockchain designed to support social media and online communities by rewarding users for creating and curating content. One of its best-known applications is Steemit, a blogging and social-media platform built on the Steem blockchain. The project's use case addresses a long-standing demand for alternatives to centralized social networks, which have often been criticized for censorship, platform control, and abrupt policy changes. However, Steem has faced significant challenges of its own over time. Steemit announced a website hack in 2016 that affected about 260 accounts, and Steemit, Inc. later laid off more than 70 percent of its staff in 2018 during the crypto bear market.

STEEM is the ecosystem's native token. The network also includes Steem Power (SP), which is used for governance and influence within the network, and Steem Dollars (SBD), a token designed to track the U.S. dollar. Steem also proposed Smart Media Tokens, or SMTs, native digital assets intended to help applications monetize content and encourage user participation.

On the technical side, Steem has long been associated with Graphene, a high-performance blockchain framework often described as a third-generation system. Historically, the Steem ecosystem supported a range of applications, including Steemit, the video-sharing platform DTube, and Utopian, which rewarded open-source contributions. DTube was originally built on Steem before later expanding beyond it, while Utopian has since been discontinued.

Let's move on to the remote viewing data for this target.

ST - Steem

The Site Template for this session follows.

11982/12394   S.T.

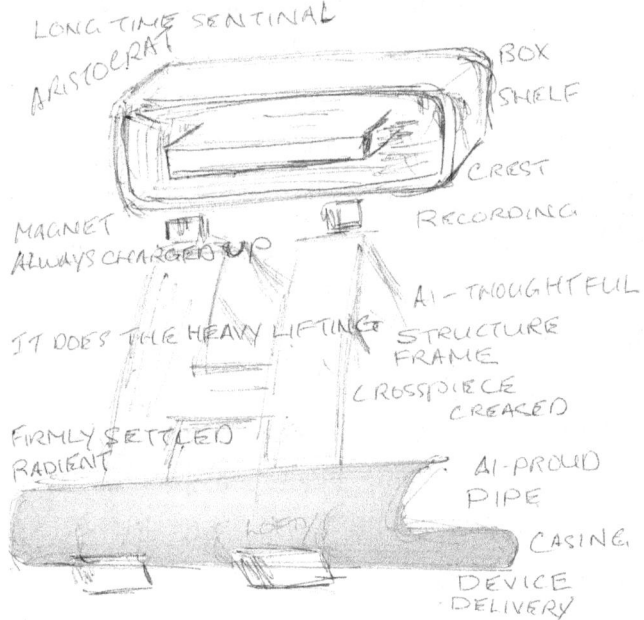

LONG TIME SENTINAL
ARISTOCRAT
AI-WONDERING
BOX
SHELF
CREST
MAGNET
ALWAYS CHARGED UP
RECORDING
IT DOES THE HEAVY LIFTING
AI-THOUGHTFUL
STRUCTURE
FRAME
CROSSPIECE
CREASED
FIRMLY SETTLED
RADIENT
AI-PROUD
PIPE
CASING
DEVICE
DELIVERY

LIKE A CARRIER PIGEON
RUNNING ALONG THE MARGIN.
STAGED

Overview of the ST Sketch

The three aspects appear to be in direct contact, or at least directly associated.

• Aspect X is a long, curving, open-looking form colored silver-gray. It sits within Aspect A.

• Aspect A resembles a trestle. Aspect X sits inside it, and Aspect B is positioned above it.

• Aspect B is an open shelf that sits at the top of Aspect A. Inside Aspect B, a long angular shape is visible.

Aspect X

A PIPE that is a DEVICE is associated with RADIANT, DELIVERY, and CASING. It is big, thin, cylindrical, dense, and hollow. There are also the ideas: LIKE A CARRIER PIGEON and RUNNING ALONG THE MARGIN.

I feel PROUD.

Aspect A

Aspect A is a long, straight, dense, gray STRUCTURE positioned vertically at an angle. It is a FRAME that forms a CROSSPIECE. It is associated with STAGED, CREASED, and LOFTY. There are also the ideas: IT DOES THE HEAVY LIFTING and FIRMLY SETTLED.

I feel THOUGHTFUL.

Aspect B

A BOX that is a SHELF is associated with RECORDING, ARISTOCRAT, CREST, and MAGNET. It is angular, open, deep, and positioned above, with evident curves. It has white and tan coloring.1

It leaves me WONDERING.

Comments on the ST

I am struck by how Aspect B, which is associated with "RECORDING," reminds me of a VHS player, and how that association fits with the purpose of DTube, the dApp created to serve video.

Aspect X, with sensories such as "RADIANT," "DELIVERY," and "LIKE A CARRIER PIGEON," aligns well with Steemit, Steem's primary platform for community-based blogging and social media. It is no surprise that Aspect X, the target aspect, corresponds to Steemit. After all, it is the most popular product in the ecosystem.

S6 - The Ultimate Future of Steem

The final page of data from the remote viewing session follows.

11982/12394   S6

CRAZY TIMES!

HOT FIREBALL

SHOCKING!

FLOATING

LIKE AN EYE LOOKING OUT.

THIS SEEMS SUPERCHARGED AND SCARY

KIWI
SESSION END @ 11:20
19 NOVEMBER 2020

The text data from the S6:

These are CRAZY TIMES!

There is a HOT FIREBALL moving to the left across the horizontal axis of the page. There is a FLOATING object appearing LIKE AN EYE LOOKING OUT.

It is SHOCKING.

THIS SEEMS SUPERCHARGED AND SCARY.

Comments and Conclusions on the S6

The S6 presents a startling image, not one I would normally associate with a decentralized social media platform.

The "hot fireball" moves in a straight line across the horizontal plane. That does not suggest a plunge to Earth. Instead, it suggests a trajectory that grazes the atmosphere and continues outward, into space. In a symbolic sense, that could be interpreted as even more significant than a "moon shot," because as we know, most of what goes up eventually comes back down.

The floating object reminds me of an electronic eye. It looks outward. Is it the "eye" itself, or its function, that feels shocking?

The phrase "supercharged and scary" gives me pause. "Scary" suggests uncertainty or risk. However, "supercharged" suggests power and purpose. "Crazy times," combined with "shocking" and "supercharged and scary," suggests that future developments may demand a cautious approach.

Perhaps Steem evolves into something unusually intense or unexpected. Either these sensories describe what Steem becomes, or they point to the conditions that drive its success. In the latter case, it may be the environment that enables Steem's success that feels scary and chaotic.

Either way, the overall picture suggests that Steem is ultimately seen as successful.

My Conclusion for Steem

I find nothing in the S6 data that suggests failure. In fact, the opposite appears true. Despite a rough start, Steem appears positioned to become something awe-inspiring. It may also head in an unanticipated direction or fill an unexpected niche.

Based on the S6 data alone, I conclude that Steem is a keeper.

AUGUR (REP)
AUGUR (REP)

About Augur

Price in USD: $16.66

Market Cap: $183,208,310

Circulating Supply: 11,000,000

[Date and Source: 04:45 UTC Tuesday, 24 November 2020; https://coinmarketcap.com/]

WP: https://www.augur.net/whitepaper.pdf

Official Website: https://www.augur.net/

Background of Augur

Augur was created to address what its developers describe as the "oracle problem": how can real-world data be brought onto a blockchain without relying on a centralized third party? Augur's answer is a decentralized prediction-market protocol built on Ethereum.

Using open-source smart contracts, Augur allows users to create and trade in peer-to-peer prediction markets on a wide range of topics, including sports, elections, financial performance, and natural events. The platform itself does not create those markets; users do. Participants buy and sell shares tied to possible outcomes and may profit either by holding positions until resolution or by trading as sentiment shifts.

Because Augur runs on Ethereum, users are exposed to Ethereum network costs, which can at times make participation expensive. However, the exact cost of using Augur varies with network conditions, so a fixed figure should be treated cautiously unless it is tied to a specific date and source.

Augur's reporting system uses REP and, in the v2 system, REPv2. Token holders report outcomes and stake tokens when doing so. Correct reporting can earn rewards from platform fees, while incorrect reporting can result in the loss of staked tokens.

Augur's logo was redesigned in 2020, even so, it retained its distinctive three-dimensional pyramid-like shape. The updated version highlights the upper facets of the diamond in bright green.

Let's move on to the remote viewing data for this target.

ST - Augur

The Site Template for this session follows.

72 CRYPTOCURRENCY REMOTE VIEWED

85338/05846   ST.

AI-INTIMIDATED

BLADE
EDGED

ROOM
STRUCTURE
EXHUMING
HAIR-CUT

BROADWAY

LOOKING AT IT LONG ENOUGH

A WAITING ROOM
IMPLANTED
ORB
PARSLEY
ANOINTED

AI-SURPRISED
NATURAL THING
SET FREE

TV
JUSTIFIED

PLACED WITH PRECISION
FIXING THE PROBLEM

SPREADING OUT

AI-PUZZLED
CAP
DOME
CARESSING
ADVANTAGEOUS

INDIGENOUS

Overview of the ST Sketch

Aspect X consists of two primary elements: an indigo, star-filled space and a gray, angular form positioned above it.

Aspect A looks like a large drooping bell-shaped flower in the ST.

Aspect B is just above the center of the ST. It is a ball surrounded by a corona. Two arrows, one straight and the other curving show Aspect B is spinning in a downward direction.

Aspect X

Aspect X consists of two primary elements: an indigo, star-filled space and a gray, angular form positioned above it.

It's enclosed inside a white-colored dark ROOM with a glistening BLADE above. There is an opening above through which I can see stars in the night sky.

This STRUCTURE is associated with EXHUMING, HAIRCUT, and BROADWAY. There are the ideas of LOOKING AT IT LONG ENOUGH and A WAITING ROOM.

It makes me feel INTIMIDATED.

. . .

Aspect A

Aspect A, resembles a large, drooping, bell-shaped cap. It forms a dome that is tall, hollow, and curving.

A tall and thick, big, curving, high, and hollow white CAP forms a DOME. It is associated with SPREADING OUT, INDIGENOUS, CARESSING, and ADVANTAGEOUS.

I am PUZZLED by it.

Aspect B

Aspect B is positioned near the center of the ST.

A NATURAL open pink-colored THING that's an ORB spinning downward in a clockwise direction. It is associated with the following sensories: PARSLEY, ANOINTED, TV, IMPLANTED, CARRIED, and JUSTIFIED.

There are also the associated ideas of PLACED WITH PRECISION, SET FREE, and FIXING THE PROBLEM.

I feel SURPRISED by it.

Comments on the ST

The structure of the ST suggests the following:

- **Aspect A**, with its themes of spreading out and advantage, correspond to Augur's native tokens—REP and REPv2—whose purpose is tied to influence, governance, and broader participation.
- **Aspect B**, the descending orb, appears to pass through or near the blade-like structure of **Aspect X**.
- This imagery is consistent with the process of creating a market, placing a precise bet, releasing it, and letting it be carried through the system.
- The impression of a "haircut" associated with Aspect X aligns symbolically with Augur's high transaction costs, which "cut away" a significant portion of user funds. It also parallels the reality that, in any prediction market, some users lose their stake

Aspect A's masking effect, and the emotional overwhelm it creates, may reflect the complexity of Augur's ecosystem and its impact on user perception.

S6 - The Ultimate Future of Augur

The final page of data from the remote viewing session follows.

85338/05846   S6.

HELD UP FOR ALL TO SEE.

LIGHTING THE WAY

PEOPLE LOOKING

VERY DISTINCT

LOOKING ON

ACUTELY JUDGEMENTAL!

SEVERAL LAYERS TO GO.

ADMIRING.

STANDING AROUND

KIWI.
SESSION END @ 18:43 AEST
19 NOV. 2020

Overview of the S6 Sketch

The text data from the S6:

The S6 is dominated by a diamond-like symbol that recalls the Augur logo. The diamond floats between angular structures above and a curved form below. It appears elevated, unsupported, and prominently displayed. People are shown looking up at it.

- There is HELD UP FOR ALL TO SEE.
- There is LIGHTING THE WAY.
- Around the central diamond shape, there are PEOPLE LOOKING.
- There is LOOKING ON.
- There is VERY DISTINCT.
- Below the point of the diamond, there's ACUTELY JUDGMENTAL!
- There are SEVERAL LAYERS TO GO.
- There is ADMIRING.
- There are people STANDING AROUND.

Comments and Conclusions on the S6

The floating diamond symbol suggests visibility, recognition, and a distinct presence.

It is clearly identifiable to many observers, and the crowd imagery indicates strong public attention.

The impressions of *"admiration," "lighting the way,"* and *"held up for all to see"* point to Augur achieving a level of prominence or respectability.

The reference to *"several layers to go"* may indicate continued development or complexity ahead.

Overall, the S6 suggests a future in which Augur is active, established, recognized, and widely observed—qualities that benefit a cryptocurrency operating in a competitive market.

Conclusion for Augur

Based on the S6, Augur's ultimate future appears strong.

It is presented as a project that is active, visible, and firmly established for all to see.

It draws admiration and attention from many observers.

I conclude that Augur is a Keeper.

9
BITCOIN (BTC)

About Bitcoin

Price in USD: $18,353.61

Market Cap: $340,505,865,596

Circulating Supply: 18,552,531 (88.35% of the total supply).

[Date and Source: 04:45 UTC Tuesday, 24 November 2020; https://coinmarketcap.com/]

WP: https://bitcoin.org/bitcoin.pdf

Official Website: https://bitcoin.org/en/

Background of Bitcoin

Bitcoin launched in 2009, following the 2008 publication of the now-famous white paper released online under the pseudonym Satoshi Nakamoto. Today, Bitcoin remains the largest cryptocurrency by market capitalization and the best-known digital asset in the world. Bitcoin.org and CoinMarketCap both describe it as the first cryptocurrency to come into actual use.

Bitcoin's value does not stem merely from being first. It is also tied to scarcity. A fixed cap is built into its code: no more than 21 million bitcoins will ever exist. Current market data lists roughly 20.0 million BTC in circulation, leaving less than 1 million still to be mined.

Bitcoin is decentralized and open-source. No government or corporation owns it or directs its use; that principle lies at the heart of its founding philosophy. Transactions are designed to take place peer-to-peer, without banks or other intermediaries standing between sender and receiver.

Let's move on to the remote viewing data for this target.

ST — Site Template for Bitcoin

The Site Template for this session follows.

BITCOIN (BTC) 83

21541/18302   S.T.

AI-OVERWHELMED
HANGS LIKE A CURTAIN OVER IT ALL.

BROWN HAZE

PATTERN

HEAVY WEIGHT
'FUZZ NET'
INSPIRING
TIRING
HIDING.

LEVERING

HINGE

AI-FAMILIAR
AOI/S-ENGINE

MACHINE
DEVICE

TRAVERSING

INSTALLED

AI-ASTONISHMENT

RECIEVER

DEVICE
TOOL   OPEN

CARRYING THE SIGNAL   SERRATED EDGES

GRABBING AHOLD AND CLAMPING DOWN
FORMS AN 'X'

Overview of the ST Sketch

The Site Template sketch contains three primary aspects. These are Aspect X , which is always regarded as the target aspect, Aspect A, and Aspect B.

Aspect X

Aspect X appears shiny, black, brick-shaped, and moving downward. Throughout the session, the recurring idea of an ENGINE is strongly associated with the target aspect.

It's heavy, long, dense, blocky, and curved DEVICE that is a MACHINE. It moves down at the west end. It is associated with LEVERING, HINGE, TRAVERSING, and INSTALLED.

It feels FAMILIAR to me.

Aspect A

A thick, wide, high, GAS with looping PARTICLES that appears as a BROWN HAZE is associated with PATTERN, INSPIRING, TIRING, and HIDING. There are the ideas of HANGS LIKE A CURTAIN OVER IT ALL, 'FUZZ NET' and HEAVYWEIGHT.

It evokes a feeling of being OVERWHELMED.

Aspect B

A thin, long open DEVICE is a TOOL associated with RECEIVER. There are the ideas of GRABBING AHOLD AND CLAMPING DOWN, SERRATED EDGES, PICKING UP, CARRYING THE SIGNAL, and FORMS AN 'X'.

I feel ASTONISHED by it.

Comments on the ST

Aspect X stands out as the target, both because it is the only element depicted in black and the only one showing movement. The imagery suggests Aspect X striking down upon the peak of Aspect B, a tool or receiver. The close association between the impressions of "installed" and "receiver," along with references to clamping, picking up, and serrated edges, suggests a functional interaction between the two aspects.

Aspect A behaves as a masking element, creating confusion and emotional overwhelm during data collection. Its role remains unclear, but it appears to obscure or veil the main activity.

S6 - The Ultimate Future of Bitcoin

The final page of data from the remote viewing session follows.

BITCOIN (BTC)

21541/18302   SG

LIFT OFF!

ASTOUNDING!

A SERIOUS ADVANTAGE

EXPLOSION

SO MANY PEOPLE SURROUND IT

LEAVING THEM IN ITS WAKE

KIWI
SESSION ENDED @ 19:36 AEST
20 NOVEMBER 2020

Here is the final data page from the session. It came through with surprising intensity.

- There is LIFT-OFF!
- There is ASTOUNDING!
- There is A SERIOUS ADVANTAGE.
- There is an EXPLOSION.
- SO MANY PEOPLE SURROUND IT.
- There is LEAVING THEM IN ITS WAKE.

The sketch shows a rocket with four upward-angled prongs blasting skyward. Streams of energy spread outward like tentacles reaching across the page, penetrating deep into the S6 space. Countless people gather around the launch. A bold arrow marks the rocket's upward trajectory, emphasizing powerful momentum.

Comments and Conclusions on the S6

The rocket has a rounded shape echoing the look of the common presentation of a physical Bitcoin combined with a dramatic upward movement. Exclamation points in the data underscore the emotional intensity of observers: *lift-off* and *astonishing* excitement.

Bitcoin is clearly depicted as a focal point for a massive number of people.

The tentacle-like streams "leaving them in its wake" suggest Bitcoin's rise exerting influence across the broader crypto ecosystem. The sensory impression *a serious advantage* points to the benefits gained by those who hold it.

This is not financial advice; this is what I observe as a remote viewer.

Who, then, are the "them" left in its wake? Based on the totality of sessions in this series, it does not refer to altcoin holders. Rather, it points to critics of Bitcoin —and perhaps critics of cryptocurrency in general— who are overtaken by Bitcoin's success.

Conclusion for Bitcoin

The takeaway is clear: Bitcoin will be a major performer, perhaps unlike any other cryptocurrency. While many promising projects exist, the data for Bitcoin is unmistakably strong.

From my remote viewing perspective, Bitcoin is going to rocket. It is, without question, a Keeper.

. . .

A Post Note

When I completed the S6 and signed off the page, I braced myself for disappointment. Most crypto projects fail, and the S6 I had just produced looked incredibly optimistic. My first reaction was that it seemed almost too good to be true—perhaps a sign my conscious mind had intruded during the remote viewing session.

For this reason, I approached the cue with a sense of unease. However, the moment I saw the target was Bitcoin, my concern faded. If any cryptocurrency could match such a powerful future trajectory, it would surely be the one that started it all.

So I stand by this data without reservation, as bold it seems, and rather suspect that any Bitcoin maximalist would agree with this conclusion wholeheartedly.

GXCHAIN (GXC)

About GXChain

Price in USD: $0.428442

Market Cap: $29,990,950

Circulating Supply: 70,000,000 (70.00% of the total supply).

[Date and Source: 04:45 UTC Tuesday, 24 November 2020; https://coinmarketcap.com/]

WP: https://whitepaperdatabase.com/gxchain-gxs-whitepaper/

Official Website: https://en.gxchain.org/

Background of GXChain

GXChain launched in 2017 as a blockchain project for decentralized data exchange, designed to connect data from different platforms and organizations. The project was developed in China and positioned itself as infrastructure for the data economy, with a focus on privacy, user authorization, and permissionless exchange. Early project materials said the data exchange would not cache personal data and was intended to support authorized peer-to-peer data trading.

GXChain also presented itself as a response to a familiar online problem: individuals usually have limited control over where their personal data goes, how much is collected, and how it is used. Project descriptions emphasized user control, data authorization, and the possibility of letting people benefit from the value their data creates.

In 2019, the project ran into serious trouble when Chinese police raided and sealed the office of Hangzhou Cunxin Data Technology, the operator behind GXChain. The project later continued development: the GXChain 2.0 roadmap was underway by August 2020, and the GXChain 2.0 testnet launched in July 2021.

Blockcity was one of GXChain's early flagship dApps. It was presented as a mobile application built around digital identity, personal-data management, and community participation. In a 2019 AMA, the team said that Blockcity's face-ID verification accepted only Chinese nationality at that stage.

The original GXChain was described as a Delegated Proof-of-Stake blockchain built on Graphene. Later project materials described GXChain 2.0 as lightweight, EVM-compatible, and designed for low-cost or gas-free use. GXC tokens have been traded on major digital-asset exchanges.

Let's move on to the remote viewing data for this target.

ST - GXChain

The Site Template for this session follows.

50566/00354   ST.

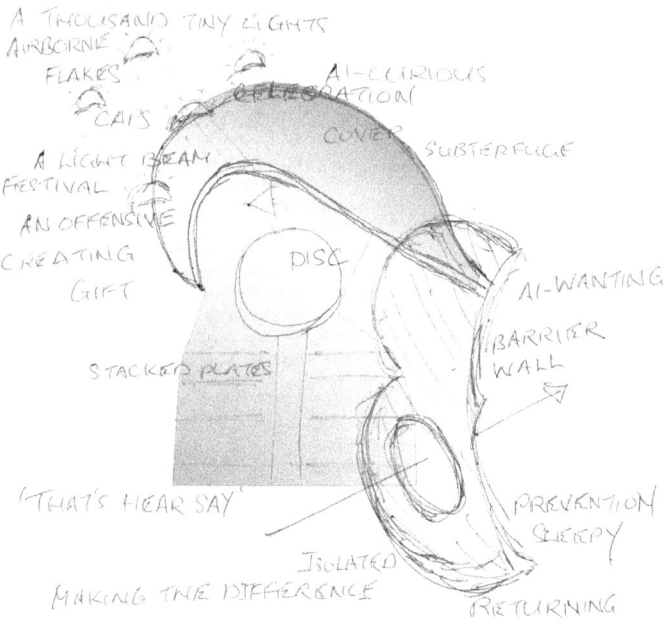

Overview of the ST Sketch

The three aspects appear closely related in the ST.

- Aspect X covers the entire blue-colored area. The curved piece at the top reminds me of the front fender of a classic motorcycle.
- Aspect A consists of many small, glowing crescents above and across Aspect X. These small objects move diagonally downward from the northwest to the southeast.
- Aspect B is curved and stands upright. It has an opening in the lower half, through which something moves from southwest to northeast, as shown by the long arrow.

Aspect X

There is a pointed, iridescent blue curved COVER. Beneath it is a DISC. The target aspect is associated with SUBTERFUGE, CREATING, and GIFT. There are STACKED PLATES below the DISC. I hear the words, "THAT'S HEARSAY."

It makes me feel CURIOUS.

· · ·

Aspect A

Small, scattered, glittery FLAKES shaped like curved CAPS move diagonally downward. They are associated with AIRBORNE, FESTIVAL, and CELEBRATIONS. Additional ideas include A THOUSAND TINY LIGHTS, A LIGHT BEAM, and AN OFFENSIVE.

It makes me feel FASCINATED.

Aspect B

A big, tall, hollow, vertically curving WALL forms a BARRIER. Aspect B is associated with PREVENTION, SLEEPY, ISOLATED, and RETURNING. There is movement through an opening in the lower half. There is also the idea of MAKING THE DIFFERENCE.

It makes me feel WANTING.

Comments on the ST

My initial reading is that Aspect A may represent user data. The "Flakes" of Aspect A move down through the curved "Cover" of Aspect X and over the "Disc" beneath it. The associated sensories suggesting festivity and light are relevant to how the system functions.

The word "Cover" is paired with "Subterfuge," which is notable. Aspect X is also associated with "Creating" and "Gift," sensories that suggest function and potential outcome.

Aspect B, the "Wall" forms a "Barrier" that prevents ("Prevention") access and keeps something "Isolated." At the same time, it contains an opening that allows significant movement to pass through. That contrast may relate to why the aspect leaves me feeling "Wanting."

The sensory "Sleepy" is unusual in this context, and "Returning" is not clearly explained by the rest of the data. My tentative interpretation is that Aspect B may relate to identity verification, or some form of authorization that restricts access while still allowing certain flows through the system. In that context, "Sleepy" could imply complacency, and "Returning" could suggest repeat users who are accustomed to the verification process.

S6 - The Ultimate Future of GXChain

The final page of data from the remote viewing session follows.

50566/00354   56.

'WE TRIED TO FIX IT'
'IT WASN'T OUR FAULT'   OLD AND NEW LEAKS.

SNOW JOB

STAINING (!)

A ROCKY WALL

GRAYSTONE

LITTLE LEFT TO SAY

KIWI
SESSION END @ 21:20 AEST
20 NOVEMBER 2020

The text data from the S6:
I can hear the words "WE TRIED TO FIX IT!"
I can hear the words "IT WASN'T OUR FAULT."
There are OLD AND NEW LEAKS.
There is a SNOW JOB.
There is STAINING IT.
There is a ROCKY WALL.
There is GRAY STONE.
There is LITTLE LEFT TO SAY.

Comments and Conclusions on the S6

There is neither color nor movement in the S6. The gray rocky wall suggests a formidable obstacle. The phrase "Old and new leaks," paired with "Staining it," suggests deterioration that has progressed over time.

"We tried to fix it" and "It wasn't our fault" read as excuses or denials. The phrase "Little left to say" reinforces a sense of reputational damage or a breakdown in credibility. "Snow job" suggests manipulation through deception, which echoes the sensory "Subterfuge" found in the ST.

Taken together, this is a bleak appraisal of GXChain's ultimate future. Based on this data, I conclude it is not a keeper.

. . .

Note on Reliability

While I aim for complete accuracy, I allow that up to thirty percent of these crypto sessions may prove incorrect. An incorrect result can occur for many reasons, including interruptions during a session or simple human variability. I am the sole remote viewer behind the raw data in these books.

To improve reliability, remote viewers often work as a team under the guidance of an experienced project manager. That is not always practical. It also does not lessen the effectiveness of a single trained remote viewer, but it does mean the data comes from one person. I encourage you to do your own analysis of the raw data, especially when you disagree with any of my conclusions.

My Conclusion for GXChain

I strongly recommend that anyone holding GXChain monitor the project closely. If you are considering the coin, be sure to research its current state before you dive in.

Considering the S6 remote viewing results, I must conclude GXChain is not a keeper.

11

CONCLUSIONS

Do these crypto projects ultimately succeed, or do they fail? After analyzing the remote viewing data, here is the short answer for each project:

- **Augur (REP)** – A success.
- **Bitcoin (BTC)** – A success. Based on the remote viewing data, I am willing to go further out on a limb on this one. BTC HODLers are going to party hard, because it will ultimately be considered a spectacular success.
- **Horizen (ZEN)** – A success, with a caveat. Stay alert for future warnings about risks associated with the project's rapid growth. Be prepared to weigh the evolving cons

against the pros. There is one big plus: looking at the data overall, I get the sense the health of the project will not become an issue.
- **GXChain (GXC)** – A fail.
- **Mimblewimblecoin (MWC)** – A success.
- **MX Token (MX)** – A fail.
- **Steem (STEEM)** – A success.
- **Yearn.Finance (YFI)** – A success.
  However, stay alert for sudden, unforeseen changes as the project grows that may lead you to reconsider whether to continue holding the cryptocurrency.

Thank you for your purchase!

Scan the QR code to leave a review or star rating on the shop page at Amazon.com.

I am excited to share the insights from my remote viewing explorations. As a reader, your perspective is invaluable, not just to me, but to other readers as well. Feedback helps books like mine find their audience, so please take a minute or two to post an honest review.

NOTES

1. Reading the Data with Ease

1. See www.crviewer.com.
2. I also use crosshatching to suggest perspective when I think position and size are critical to an aspect. This technique is used in design and architecture to good effect. I have not found that it conflicts with remote-viewing protocol.
3. Color graphics apply only to the ebook editions. Please check that your device can display color if the STs appear in black and white. At present, the ST pages in the paperback edition are printed in black and white. I would prefer them to be seen in color, as in the ebooks, but color printing would require a significant price increase to cover higher printing costs. I hope increased sales will soon support a color print edition.

2. How we do this: Horizen

1. Note for readers with a background in blockchain technology or information technology: Begin by re-identifying the raw data before attempting to interpret it.
2. Sufficient to say that ARV is used to answer binary questions. In that context, displacement describes a situation in which the remote viewer's data mixes elements of both A and B targets so thoroughly that it becomes impossible to determine which is correct.

3. MX Token (MX)

1. See: https://coinbureau.com/review/mexc-review

ALSO BY KIWI JOE

I started my Technical Remote Viewing (TRV) training in early 2010. TRV was developed by Major Ed Dames (US Army Retired). It is the next iteration of the original CRV protocol taught in the US Army to hand-picked recruits. There are several mainstream branches that stem from CRV, each with its unique flavor. They adhere to a similar step-by-step structure, a discipline distinguishing remote viewers from psychics.

If you're keen on mastering this skill, I recommend finding a teacher. Don't delay. The rewards of practicing remote viewing are significant. This is a journey of discovery that will forever change your perception of the world and yourself.

    Apart from remote viewing, I lead a typical life with my family. I hope you enjoyed the book. Be safe out there, and keep your eyes open to the possibilities.

If you have a question or suggestion you think I can respond to, please feel free to email me. I read all the correspondence I get from readers and do my best to answer promptly.
kiwijoe.rv@gmail.com

You can also find me here:
https://www.facebook.com/KiwiJoesRemoteViewing/
https://www.bookbub.com/profile/kiwi-joe

ALSO BY KIWI JOE

CLICKABLE IMAGE LINKS WILL TAKE YOU TO THE ENGLISH LANGUAGE COPIES. HOWEVER, ALL RELEASES IN MULTIPLE LANGUAGES FROM 2023.

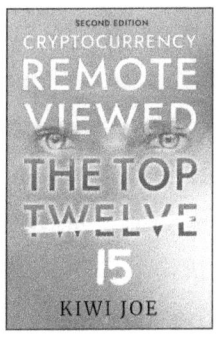

The 'Cryptocurrency Remote Viewed' series covers sixty-six cryptos. They are Kiwi Joe's top twelve picks from those he has covered so far. They include an additional bonus coin, and because this is the 2nd edition, another three cryptos! You will be surprised at the bargains available in this volatile market. These coins and tokens are deemed worthy of HODLing based solely on Joe's analysis of the remote viewing data.

ALSO BY KIWI JOE

Book Seven is packed full of background and remote viewing data, guiding readers on what to search for in more conventional information sources. This book targets seasoned remote viewers, cryptocurrency enthusiasts, and those seeking a research edge in crypto projects.

The book delves into twelve coins and tokens, each chapter detailing its background and its future as revealed by my remote viewing. The remote viewing information offers insights into crypto projects that traditional sources might overlook. Each chapter concludes with a definitive statement on the cryptocurrency's long-term viability based on remote viewing results.

The cryptocurrencies covered in this book are as follows:

- **Ankr (ANKR)**
- **Dash (DASH)**
- **Decred (DCR)**
- **Fantom (FTM)**
- **GateToken (GT)**
- **Handshake (HNS)**

- **Hive (HIVE)**
- **Maker (MKR)**
- **SingularityNET (AGIX)**
- **Terra (LUNA)**
- **Unibright (UBT)**
- **Wanchain (WAN)**

ALSO BY KIWI JOE

Book Six further expands the series with a deeper dive into the background of each project than is found in the previous books. There is also an extended analysis of the remote viewing data along with supplementary sections for added clarity and detail. The coins covered are the following:

- **Ark (ARK)**
- **Binance Coin (BNB)**
- **Bitcoin Gold (BTG)**
- **Bitshares (BTS)**
- **EOS (EOS)**
- **Mysterium (MYST)**
- **OXEN (OXEN)**
- **Reserve Rights (RSR)**
- **SERUM (SRM)**
- **STORJ (STORJ)**
- **SushiSwap (SUSHI)**
- **TomoChain (TOMO)**

ALSO BY KIWI JOE

Book Six further expands the series with a deeper dive into the background of each project than is found in the previous books. There is also an extended analysis of the remote viewing data along with supplementary sections for added clarity and detail. The coins covered are the following:

- **Ark (ARK)**
- **Binance Coin (BNB)**
- **Bitcoin Gold (BTG)**
- **Bitshares (BTS)**
- **EOS (EOS)**
- **Mysterium (MYST)**
- **OXEN (OXEN)**
- **Reserve Rights (RSR)**
- **SERUM (SRM)**
- **STORJ (STORJ)**
- **SushiSwap (SUSHI)**
- **TomoChain (TOMO)**

- **Hive (HIVE)**
- **Maker (MKR)**
- **SingularityNET (AGIX)**
- **Terra (LUNA)**
- **Unibright (UBT)**
- **Wanchain (WAN)**

ALSO BY KIWI JOE

Book Five evaluates the performance of the targeted cryptos and covers ten remote viewing sessions. He tells you which of the coins below are the long-term winners and which are the losers.

- **Celo (CELO)**
- **Gnosis (GNO)**
- **Loopring (LRC)**
- **MonaCoin (MONA)**
- **Monero (XMR)**
- **NEAR Protocol (NEAR)**
- **Numeraire (NMR)**
- **RedFOX Labs (RFOX)**
- **Streamr (DATA)**
- **SwissBorg (CHSB)**

Remote viewing focuses solely on the truth. All the cryptos covered in the series are taken from a blind target pool compiled from the top 190 as ranked according to market cap in late October 2020. The use of a blind pool is the standard approach remote viewers take to avoid corrupting their session by having foreknowledge of the target.

In Book Four the remote viewing sessions reveals the winners and losers among the following coins:

- **Ardor (ARDR)**
- **Basic Attention Token (BAT)**
- **Cronos (CRO)**
- **Nano (NANO)**
- **Orchid (OXT)**
- **Theta Fuel (TFUEL)**
- **Thunder Token (TT)**
- **TitanSwap (TITAN)**
- **XRP (XRP)**
- **Zilliqa (ZIL)**

ALSO BY KIWI JOE

Book Three offers a chapter guiding newcomers on how to analyze remote viewing data.

The book reveals the winners and losers according to the remote viewing data among the following coins:

- **Adex Network (ADX)**
- **Aeternity (AE)**
- **RSK Infrastructure Framework (RIF)**
- **Solana (SOL)**
- **Synthetix (SNX)**
- **Switcheo (SWTH)**
- **Xinfin Network (XDC)**
- **Neo (NEO)**

ALSO BY KIWI JOE

Book Two showcases some essential remote viewing sessions with Kiwi Joe targeting eight cryptos, one of which is Bitcoin. In addition, in the 'How We Do This' chapter, the book demonstrates aspects of remote viewing analysis in more detail using the crypto project Horizen as an example. The following coins and tokens are covered in the book:

- **Augur (REP)**
- **Bitcoin (BTC)**
- **Gxchain (GXC)**
- **Horizen (ZEN)**
- **Mimblewimblecoin (MWC)**
- **Mx Token (MX)**
- **Steem (STEEM)**
- **Yearn.Finance (YFI)**

ALSO BY KIWI JOE

Cryptos are soaring, but there are surprises to come. Some will be not so good, and some will be very good. This series uses remote viewing to predict the ultimate future for various cryptos. It shows you the winners and the losers, and for the latter, it's those crypto-assets you should take a good hard look at before you leap in. Only remote viewing gives you this kind of pre-warning.

"Cryptocurrency Remote Viewed Book One" is available for FREE download (i.e., the ebook).

Discover what the future has in store for the following cryptos:

- **Chainlink (LINK)**
- **Hxro (HXRO)**
- **Kusama (KSM)**
- **Tron (TRX)**
- **Uniswap (UNI)**
- **Velas (VLX)**

ALSO BY KIWI JOE

This is the 2nd Edition of 'Most Secret Weapons of Nations Remote Viewed'—Book IV in the Remote Viewed series. Guaranteed to fascinate and disturb you, in turn. All the targets explored were drawn from a blind pool used by Kiwi Joe in practice sessions over a period of six years. They comprise eighteen sessions covering ten countries. Nine of the ten weapons remain secret with two of them hidden in plain sight.

As you might expect from a book on the subject, it contains some startling and troubling information. One of its conclusions is that the entire globe is now a battlefield. The original sketches from the remote viewing sessions illustrate the book. Read it now, if you dare.

The question of how we address the continuing radioactive seep from the disabled Nuclear Power Plant has been remote viewed and the answer found. The bad news is that the sheer scale of the project presents a real challenge to engineers. The good news is that it can be done, so long as there exists the will to do it. The problem of scale did not deter the ancients from building the pyramids of Giza. So, we know stopping the radiation leak at the Daiichi Power Plant can be done.

Ironically, in light of the above, Japan is considering a proposal to build the gigantic Shimizu Mega-City Pyramid over Tokyo Bay. The concept was first made public just three years after the Fukushima Daiichi meltdowns, which seems to raise a question of priorities. The economic welfare of a nation is critical to its population's health, but isn't the health of the nation also reliant on the well-being of its people?

In 2012, Kiwi Joe was a member of a remote viewing team blind tasked to find the best solution. While the work done by the rest of the team can't be included in this book, the vast majority of that data lines up with what he gathered in his remote viewing sessions. This book outlines the necessary steps and offers observations based on analysis of the remote viewing data.

The book is illustrated with drawings from two remote viewing sessions completed while Kiwi Joe was part of the team. It includes the final session, which resembles a blueprint. It shows the three main steps needed. Along with endnotes citing the sources used in writing the background for this book, there is a resource list for those who want more information about remote viewing. The author includes his contact details in the back if readers have questions or suggestions for him.

Important update: Forrest Fenn confirmed the treasure chest's discovery to the Santa Fe New Mexican on June 07, 2020. Congratulations to the finder!

This book marks the second installment in the Remote Viewed series. It covers many remote viewing sessions that targeted the location of Forrest Fenn's treasure chest. The book aimed to help readers verify solutions and strategies, rethink them where necessary, and pose critical questions they may not otherwise have considered.

Kiwi Joe explains the meaning of two of the most important clues in Forrest Fenn's poem, and shows the location of the chest within a one-and-a-half-mile radius. He also provides a bird's-eye view and perspectives from higher altitudes. Finally, he shows how the data points to the specific region in the Rocky Mountains.

There are 21 illustrations in total taken from six extended remote view sessions. Additionally, there's a resource list including literature and online sources. There is something for both treasure hunters and remote viewers alike.

ALSO BY KIWI JOE

Important update: Forrest Fenn confirmed the treasure chest's discovery to the Santa Fe New Mexican on June 07, 2020. Congratulations to the finder!

Kiwi Joe was on the lookout for a suitable popular mystery to demonstrate the power of remote viewing. Mr. Fenn's treasure hunt was perfect for the project, and with the agreement of his client, he released two books using the session work he had completed for himself. The detailed remote viewing maps and accompanying data are significant for treasure hunters.

This first book alone offered significant information to decode Forrest Fenn's cryptic clues, verify solutions and strategies, and prompt rethinking where necessary. The book reveals how Mr. Fenn positioned the chest so that a treasure hunter close to the site could throw a rock at it.

There is a bird's eye view of the immediate area, and as a bonus, Kiwi Joe gives the reader a peek inside the chest.

The book includes 16 full-page illustrations from five remote view sessions and the analysis of the data with conclusions. Additionally, there's a resource list of relevant literature as well as other online sources for both treasure hunters and remote viewers. The book is divided into two parts, with all illustrations in the second part.

with conclusions. Additionally, there's a resource list of relevant literature as well as other online sources for both treasure hunters and remote viewers. The book is divided into two parts, with all illustrations in the second part.

BIBLIOGRAPHY

NB: The list is far from comprehensive, but it does give an idea of the range of publications on the subject of Remote Viewing.

Remote Viewing

Brown, C. (2005). *Remote Viewing: The Science and Theory of Nonphysical Perception.*

Buchanan, L. (2003). *The Seventh Sense: The Secrets of Remote Viewing as Told by a "Psychic Spy" for the US Military.*

Dames, E. (2010). *Tell Me What You See: Remote Viewing Cases from the World's Premier Psychic Spy.*

Knowles, J. (2017). *Remote Viewing from the Ground Up.*

William, L. L. (2017). *Monitoring: A Guide for Remote Viewing & Professional Intuitive Teams.*

Marrs, J. (2007). *PSI Spies: The True Story of America's Psychic Warfare Program.*

McMoneagle, J. (2000). *Remote Viewing Secrets: A Handbook for extending and developing your psychic abilities.*

Morehouse, D. (1998). *Psychic Warrior: Inside the CIA's Stargate Program: The True Story of a Soldier's Espionage and Awakening.*

Noble, J., & Coronado, Pam. (2018). *Natural Remote Viewing: A practical guide to the mental martial art of self-discovery.*

Puthoff, H. E. (2002). Searching for the Universal Matrix in Metaphysics. *Research New and Opportunities and Theology*, 2(8).

Rifat, T. (2003). *Remote Viewing: What it is, Who Uses it and How to do it*

Ronson, J. (2005). *The Men Who Stare at Goats.*

Schwartz, S. A. (1976). *The Secret Vaults of Time: Psychic Archaeology and the Quest for Man's Beginnings.*

Smith, D. (2013). *CRV - Controlled Remote Viewing: Manuals, collected papers & information to help you learn Controlled Remote Viewing.*

Smith, D. (2015). *Remote Viewing Dialogues: Psychic Spy Veterans from the 23 Year, US Military and Intelligence Remote Viewing Programs, Share their Expertise.*

Smith, P. (2005). *Reading the Enemy's Mind: Inside Star Gate: America's Psychic Espionage Program.*

Smith, P. H., & Feather, Sally Rhine. (2015). *The Essential Guide to Remote Viewing: The Secret Military Remote Perception Skill Anyone Can Learn.*

Stuart, B. (2016). *Technical Remote Viewing: The Complete Guide.*

Swann, I. (2018). *Everybody's Guide to Natural ESP.*

Swann, I. (2018). *Penetration: The Question of Extraterrestrial and Human Telepathy.*

Targ, R. (2004). *Limitless Mind: A Guide to Remote Viewing and Transformation of Consciousness.*

Targ, R. (2012). *The Reality of ESP: A Physicists's Proof of Psychic Abilities.*

Thompson Smith, A. (2019). *Tactical Remote Viewing.*

Vivanco, J. (2016). *The Time Before the Secret Words: On the path of remote viewing, high strangeness and zen.*